"I used these ideas in class and had a wonderful day with my students."

Thank you so much!! I used these ideas in class and had a wonderful day with my students. As a first Year Relief Teacher I find this site invaluable in helping me become a better and more confident Teacher.

Jess (Take Control of the Noisy Class customer)

* * *

"It is very rewarding to see a teacher apply strategies from Rob's materials, then get excited as they see the 'magic' work."

"The materials have been right on target, students have benefitted as well as teachers. It is very rewarding to see a teacher apply strategies from Rob's materials, then get excited as they see the 'magic' work. Thank you for making my job easier and validating the experience."

Cheryl E. Le Fon (Take Control of the Noisy Class customer)

Classroom Management Success

in 7 Days or Less

Needs-Focused Teaching Resource Book 1

Rob Plevin

http://www.needsfocusedteaching.com

About the Author

Rob Plevin is an ex-deputy head teacher and Special Education Teacher with the practical experience to help teachers in today's toughest classrooms.

No stranger to behaviour management issues, Rob was 'asked to leave' school as a teenager. Despite his rocky route through the education system he managed to follow his dream of becoming a teacher after spending several years working as an outdoor instructor, corporate trainer and youth worker for young people in crisis. Since then he has worked with challenging young people in residential settings, care units and tough schools and was most recently employed as Deputy Head at a PRU for children and teenagers with behaviour problems. He was identified as a key player in the team which turned the unit round from 'Special Measures'.

He now runs needsfocusedteaching.com, is the author of several books and presents training courses internationally for teachers, lecturers, parents and care workers on behaviour management & motivation. His live courses are frequently described as 'unforgettable' and he was rated as an 'outstanding' teacher by the UK's Office for Standards in Education.

Rob's courses and resources feature the Needs-Focused Approach™ – a very effective system for preventing and dealing with behaviour problems in which positive staff/student relationships are given highest priority.

To book Rob for INSET or to enquire about live training please visit the help desk at

www.needsfocusedteaching.com

Introduction

Free bonus materials & printable resources

This book, like the others in this series, is for teachers like you who want to connect and succeed with tough, hard-to-reach students in the shortest possible time. To help you do this, it comes complete with additional bonus material as well as printable resources to accompany the activities explained in the book.

Wherever you see the **'resource icon'** in this book, head over to our website to get your free resources and accompanying printables,

Please visit:

http://needsfocusedteaching.com/kindle/transform/

About the Book

'Classroom Management Success' is book #1 in my Needs-Focused Teaching Resource series. This collection of teaching books is my attempt to provide teachers with practical, fast-acting, tried-and-tested strategies and resources that work in today's toughest schools. The novel, quirky ideas and methods form part of my Needs Focused Approach and have been tried and tested with hard-to-reach, reluctant learners of all ages, in more than 40 countries. Over the last 10 years or more they have been found to be highly effective in improving learning, raising achievement, building trusting relationships and creating positive learning environments.

Each book in this series includes a comprehensive suite of bonus materials and printable resources as I want to give you as much support as possible and for you to be delighted with your book purchase. Please be sure to download your bonus resources from my website here:

http://needsfocusedteaching.com/kindle/transform/

* * *

Here's what you'll find in these pages:

a) A very simple and logical explanation as to why you currently experience behaviour problems in your lessons,

b) A very simple, logical way of preventing them, and

c) A set of strategies which, when applied, can dramatically improve behaviour in your classroom in a week or less.

But before we get into it, let me take a moment to tell you why I wrote this little book.

I first wrote it several years ago when my teacher training business, Behaviour Needs, was doing incredibly well. At the time, we were one of the best-known behaviour-related websites (ranking at #1 for the term 'classroom management') and I was travelling all over the world delivering training to teachers, university lecturers, parents and carers. Our videos & resources we're being downloaded thousands of times a day. Actually, if you type 'classroom management' into the search box on YouTube right now, some 5 years later, you'll see that we're still at the top of the charts with a video that has had well over a million views. But my situation is very different now.

In 2010, my wife and I were almost killed in an unprovoked knife attack which ultimately led to us dramatically reassessing things. After several painful and draining years fighting to keep my training business afloat I realised I was burned out and reluctantly had to let it go. I retrained as a mindfulness & meditation teacher, as this was the only tool I could find that gave me freedom from the horror of Post-Traumatic Stress, and this sparked a new, more relaxed, direction for my life.

I had no intention of returning to teacher training – as most of my time is now spent teaching meditation and mindfulness (you can find me at www.theliferaft.org) - but I quickly became inundated with requests to carry on producing the novel, quirky and practical resources I had become known for through Behaviour Needs.

I finally decided to make my materials available under a new brand – www.needsFocusedTeaching.com - where you can find many of my courses and resources. These days I prefer to run online learning programs instead of travelling and setting up live workshops. I still run occasional INSET sessions although I have very limited availability.

I recently compiled most of my best strategies into two main volumes – Take Control of the Noisy Class (published by Crown House and available on Amazon in paperback and Kindle formats) – and Motivate the Unmotivated (published by my publishing company, Life Raft Media and available through Amazon). In addition, many of my other titles are now available on the Kindle platform and in Paperback. Just do a search for me on Amazon and you'll see my full range.

Classroom Management Success in 7 Days or Less is an introduction to my Needs-Focused Approach which I'll tell you more about in a minute. I wanted to make the book available at low cost, partly because I love helping teachers – I've been doing it a long time and love the feedback I receive - and partly because, being totally open and honest with you, I want to draw your attention to my other books in the hope that you'll buy them. Cheeky, I know. But if you like what you find here, you'll absolutely LOVE my other titles.

Even though this is only an introductory guide, it contains some deceptively powerful strategies and ideas and each section includes links to download additional resources from my website. There is no charge for these bonus resources – I genuinely want you to benefit from this book.

Make no mistake, the strategies I'm sharing *work*. And even if you feel you're already aware of some of them, please try applying them before dismissing them. I didn't choose the title lightly; these ideas completely and quickly transformed my ability to manage tough groups and individuals early in my career and I don't think I would have survived, let alone done so well in some of the settings I worked in were it not for the techniques I'm sharing here.

I believe passionately and wholeheartedly that meeting students' innate psychological needs – particularly in terms of building positive relationships with them and acknowledging their efforts – is fundamental to gaining their trust and respect. From there you can teach them, help them grow, influence them in positive ways and help them succeed. Without that foundation of trust and respect your job will be a series of battles from bell to bell in which nobody wins.

The Needs Focused Approach

So, what is the Needs Focused Approach and how can it help you? Well, it's based on Abraham Maslow's Hierarchy of Needs theory which suggests that humans share a wide range of emotional and psychological needs – from the need to achieve through the need to contribute, to the need for love and a whole host of others in between.

The Needs-Focused Approach breaks down these psychological needs into just three broad groups to make life easy. Let me explain what the three groups are and why they are so crucially important in terms of both preventing problems, and responding to students who misbehave. The first group of needs falls under the heading 'Empowerment' and includes things like recognition, freedom, autonomy, achievement, contribution, choice and competence. Second is the need for 'Fun' and includes curiosity, interest, growth and learning, adventure, amusement, surprise, variety. Finally, is the need to 'Belong' – to be accepted, valued, appreciated, needed, related to or connected with something beyond oneself.

If you think about it, few of us function well without adequate control, choice, autonomy and freedom in our lives - we need to be *empowered*. We can't live happy lives without at least some variety, humour, activity or *fun*. And we feel isolated and alone if we're not valued or appreciated by others or connected to them in some way - we need to *belong*. When these three needs are NOT being met - when they are missing from our lives - we tend to feel frustrated and unsettled. That's when the problems start.

Consider the following scenario: imagine if you will, a thoroughly *boring* lesson. You know the type I mean – a teacher handing out worksheet after worksheet, standing at the front of the room, like a shop-window dummy going through the motions.

There's no engaging warm-up activity to grab the students' attention, no variety or choice in terms of lesson tasks or level of challenge, no novelty or intrigue, no humour, no laughter, no sense of discovery, no interaction or movement around the room, no music, no curious props, no energiser, no recognition or praise for efforts made and no attention given to differing learning styles. It's the kind of lesson that makes kids want to get up and walk out.

What usually happens in a lesson like this? You guessed it: students misbehave. It might start with fairly innocent activities such as doodling or passing notes, but left unchecked the activities become increasingly disruptive: getting up and walking around, throwing things, shouting silly comments, dishing abuse to the teacher, not doing work, tapping pencils, refusing to follow instructions, dictating their own terms, using mobile phones etc. What has resulted is the typical behaviour problems arising from frustration and dissatisfaction – from *needs that have not been met*.

Remember, our psychological needs are *crucial* to us and must be satisfied – they are a primeval, subconscious thirst which *must* be quenched and as important to us as water and sunlight are to a plant. If the teacher doesn't provide a means to meet these needs as part of regular day-to-day practice, students will seek satisfaction in less appropriate ways of their own devising. In other words, if you don't give them fun, they'll make their own. If you don't give them a sense of power, they will assert themselves in their own way. And if you don't make them feel valued they will opt out and form trouble-making splinter groups. (Have you ever wondered why 'gangs' are so appealing to young people?)

Throughout this little book, I will present ways of satisfying these three key needs in order to help you prevent a large proportion of problems from ever arising in your classroom. I'll also show you how to respond to misbehaviour in ways that promote respect from miscreants rather than stirring them up and causing confrontation.

I don't claim that *all* your problems will be solved but by adopting the strategies and ideas that follow you will *definitely* see a dramatic reduction in the number of incidents you're currently dealing with on a daily basis. And I guarantee the improvements will appear within a few days. We're going to look at ways of making students feel a sense of belonging – by making them feel part of the classroom community, by strengthening peer relationships and by building positive, mutually respectful student-teacher bonds. It makes a huge difference to struggling, troubled (and troublesome) students to feel accepted, welcomed and valued in school.

We will look at ways of <u>empowering</u> students by providing them with realistic chances to achieve and experience success, by giving them a degree of autonomy and choice and by ensuring their efforts are recognised and acknowledged. Again, this comes down to making students feel valued as well as giving them confidence in their abilities to attempt and complete lesson tasks. Many behaviour problems can be attributed to students feeling *inadequate* in the school environment. Even outwardly tough young people are fearful of making a fool of themselves in front of others and this is why they opt out, argue and mess around – it's often nothing more than classic work avoidance.

And we will look at ways of improving motivation in lessons by making lessons more interactive and appealing, more stimulating, more relevant and more <u>fun</u>. Now and again you can be forgiven for having a lesson of bookwork or worksheets. Now and again you can be forgiven for a lack-lustre performance and for not displaying your usual enthusiasm and love for your subject. No problem there, that's life. The problems arise when the *majority* of lessons all follow the same format. If there is a continual lack of challenge, a continual lack of variety and a continual lack of novelty there will almost certainly be a continual lack of interest from the students.

Now, without further ado, let's get started...

Part 1.

Satisfying the Need to Belong – Building Positive Staff/ Student Relationships

Let's kick things off with a little puzzle:

Mr. Jones is looking for a teaching job and sees vacancies advertised at two very different inner-city schools within the same catchment area. School A has a perfect behaviour management policy – it has comprehensive, consistent systems and procedures in place as well as a clearly defined hierarchy of rewards and sanctions. School B is undergoing some changes and has no real policy for managing behaviour. Staff have no clear guidelines in terms of what constitutes suitable rewards or what to do in response to the range of behaviour problems they encounter.

Question: In which school would Mr. Jones find it easiest to manage behaviour?

Answer: See end of this section *after* reading the rest of this chapter.

There are several reasons why I believe positive staff-student relationships to be so important. For one thing, when you really get to know a student you become aware of their triggers - the things that upset them and result in problems in class. And when you're dealing with children who carry all kinds of emotional baggage and flare up for no apparent reason, this is *vital*. You know what to look out for and can plan accordingly. Stopping behaviour problems from occurring is much easier when you know what causes them.

Secondly, when you reach out and get to know any child in school you show them they're *valued*. Kids need to feel valued, supported, loved.

Once they see that you're there for them and respect them as individuals they will, in turn, respect and trust you. They will respond more positively to a teacher they trust and respect.

Thirdly, when you form positive relationships with your students their ability to take an active role in *other* positive relationships is improved; they fit in better with their peers and so are less likely to need to 'act up' to get attention.

The problem is, how do we go about building relationships with challenging students? It's fine talking about all this – most people in education agree that this is crucial stuff - but how do we actually make it happen rather than just play lip service to it?

Well, if you think about it all relationships have *communication* at their heart. You can't have a relationship of any kind unless communication is involved in some form so it's not surprising we have poor relationships with our most challenging students; they're usually among the last people we 'chat along nicely' with.

Clearly, if we're going to build a relationship with them we need to get them talking but as you've no-doubt discovered, getting them to open up and *wanting* to talk is a huge hurdle to overcome. Striking up a conversation with your average, maladjusted 14 year old is difficult, especially when you don't know them very well. It's a vicious circle: you can't get to know them until you have something to talk about, and you have little to talk about with them until you get to know them better.

There is a simple solution to this dilemma though and it's so obvious you'll kick yourself if you haven't already worked out the answer. All you have to do is **find out what interests them.**

People enjoy talking about things they're actually interested in and your students, even the most challenging ones, are no different. Once you know their passions you can easily strike up conversation with them - you have a subject to chat about which will engage and excite them.

For example, if their favourite subject turns out to be 'mountain biking' you could:

- Ask their advice about new bikes or related equipment (we all like to be able to show how knowledgeable we are about a subject, particularly if it's our *favourite* one. Don't get me started about quinoa.)

- Share stories you've seen on television about mountain biking.

- Make up a list of websites on mountain biking - "Here Jonny, you said you were into mountain biking, I found these websites you might like to look at..."

- Find old books/magazines or newspaper clippings and offer them as a something to look at in their spare time.

- Ask them about their bike or their riding adventures – perhaps they ride in competitions.

- Ask their advice on local tracks or courses

- Take your own bike into school and ask them to show you how to fix it (Remember: people LOVE being given opportunity to show their expertise)

- Sell them that old bike you never got round to putting on Ebay.

The problem, of course, is finding out what their hobbies and interests are in the first place. So how do we discover these?

OK, we could just *ask them* but as we know already, they may not be too keen to open up if we have no relationship in place to start with. We need a *less invasive* way of discovering their interests and it just so happens that I've got one for you which I've relied on many times throughout my career. I got the idea from my dear, late father. He was a wise man and his advice was always reliable so you can use it with confidence. I call it the **Record Card Questionnaire.**

Record Cards are used by salesmen to record a client's personal information so he can be more familiar on his next visit. Each time he returns to the same client and has a conversation, more information is recorded on the card. These tidbits gradually build up and form a library of useful information which can be drawn on during the next meeting and gradually the relationship develops as the client and salesman have more to talk about. It just speeds up the natural process of trust-building and information sharing which would otherwise take much longer. It's obvious to see that the salesman who does this will get on better with his client and probably sell more – even if he sells double glazing! For example...

Salesman A (Who has spent time recording his client's personal details on his Record Card):

"Hey John how are you this week? How's Lillian? You haven't forgotten her birthday on Friday, have you? I brought you this booklet on carpet cleaning after your little accident last week. Now then, shall I show you this new line?"

Salesman B (Who has taken no interest in his client):

"Hello Mr Smith. Would you like to buy our new product? No? Oh okay, bye then."

You can see from this example that the record card is a great way of reducing the time normally spent getting to know someone and we can adapt this idea for classroom use simply by giving students a fun questionnaire. They can complete this in registration periods, free periods, break times, 'getting to know you' sessions, social skills lessons, as an 'early finisher' exercise etc.

There's not a lot to it – it's just a collection of fairly innocent questions that will appeal to a young person's imagination. And to help you out, I've got one for you to download. The version I'm giving you is one I used for years in all kinds of settings. With some minor tweaks, you can adapt it for virtually any age group.

<u>BONUS TOOL:</u> Record Card Questionnaire

 You can find a copy to download on our website here:

<u>http://needsfocusedteaching.com/kindle/ transform/</u>

What do you do with the completed questionnaires?

The information you glean from these documents can be used in a variety of relationship-enhancing ways such as...

• Increase the effectiveness of **spontaneous rewards** by tailoring them to appeal to students' interests. For example, if you have a student who's nuts about a certain breed of dog, there's no point in giving her a sticker with a car on it! (You'll find out more about 'Spontaneous Rewards' later).

• Provide appealing **reading material** for break times, quiet reading sessions, registration - magazines, journals and books that relate to their specific areas of interest.

• Plan really **interesting lessons**. You might choose to plan a series of lessons for the whole class around a topic that several students are interested in, or cover a skill such as narrative writing and encourage them to write a story about their subject of interest.

• Use them as a **conversation starter**. They enable you to strike up conversation on a topic you know they're interested in and this is crucial with 'hard to reach' kids - it shows you care about them and are interested in them.

I know you're probably thinking that collating all those questionnaires is going to take a lot of time but please remember you *don't* have to do this with every student you work with.

The idea is to focus on building bonds with *your most challenging students*. Most of the members of your class will naturally find a sense of belonging in school – we need to concentrate on those who don't. That's not to say we ignore the other students, they still need and deserve our attention and support, it's just that we need to work a bit harder to include those who struggle to fit in and who subsequently misbehave.

Show them you care

OK, once you've started communicating with your students more frequently, the next step on your relationship-building journey is to introduce the second key feature of any positive relationship – showing that you care about them. Again, it's impossible to build a warm, positive relationship with anyone unless you express a level of care and appreciation towards them – they need to know you actually *like* them.

For some teachers, this notion is worrying so let me be clear on this – I'm NOT suggesting you try to be their 'friend'. Do that and, at best, you can end up looking unprofessional. At worst, you can quickly get a reputation as a pathetic walkover and will struggle with *any* group from then on. No, I'm not saying you should be their *friend* but you should always try to be friend-*ly*. There is a big difference.

Now, if you'd like some proven, fast-acting ways to convince your students that you care about them and have their best interests at heart I've got you covered. I've put 5 of my best methods together for you in a short download imaginatively titled **'5 Ways to Show Students You Care'** and you can get your copy from the resources page I've set up for you here:

 http://needsfocusedteaching.com/kindle/transform/

Positive teacher-student relationships are, in my opinion, the *only* classroom management tool you really need. The teacher who can connect & build bonds with young people will never have problems with student behaviour. I've watched teachers who are good at this work in temporary classrooms in porta-cabins with next to no resources, with no support from senior management, no school-wide systems and no behavior management policy in place.

Despite these issues (which many teachers would find intolerable) they are able to thrive. They can do so in *any* setting with *any* child simply because they make relationships a priority. Bottom line – children will behave better for a teacher they like, trust and get on well with. It's not rocket science, is it?

So... please download your free resources and start building relationships with your students if this isn't already a priority for you. I promise it will make a huge difference.

And now, here's the answer to the little quiz question...

A. Obviously, we can't give an answer with the information available. Although we are given some details about the school we are given no information about what sort of teacher Mr. Jones is. He may possess no real skills in terms of getting along with challenging students.

He might not even like kids that much. If that's the case, if he isn't prepared to reach out and build bonds with these students and is negative towards them it doesn't matter how good the school system is – he will fail.

On the other hand, if his approach towards the students suggests he is there for them, there to help and support them, interested in them and keen to see them succeed come what may, there is a good chance they will respond positively towards him – no matter how poor or ineffective the system is. Positive staff-student relationships make classroom management *much* easier.

Part 2

Satisfying the Need to Belong – Building Classroom Community

OK, we've looked at developing staff-student relationships as a way of meeting students' need for belonging; let's look at another one now – building classroom community. Students work best and cause least problems when they feel they are part of a *community* in which they feel accepted and in which their individuality is encouraged.

By definition a community is a group of people who work with one another building a sense of trust, care, and support. This means that in our classrooms, part of our job is to provide opportunities and structures by which students can work collaboratively and support and help one another.

Here are two good ways to build classroom community: Student Meetings and Team-Building activities.

1. Student Meetings

Student meetings are valuable tools for handling issues that arise and for finding out what is working for your students, and for seeking ideas about how things can improve in areas that are *not* working. They are also perfect for building teacher-student bonds. Meetings can be arranged on a 1:1 basis or by assigning students to small 'focus groups' of 4-5.

During a student meeting the main objective is to convince students that this is an opportunity for them to have a <u>*voice*</u> - a chance to talk about issues which are bothering them and to put forward <u>their own ideas</u> for how things could improve.

It's vitally important to remember the purpose of the meetings is *not* to apportion blame or complain about lack of work. Rather, the aim is to solicit ideas for improvement from the students and to talk about what is working ("we'll do more of these activities...") and what isn't working ("we'll do fewer of these activities.... or seek to improve them").

Meetings need only be 10-20 minutes long – little more than a quick summary of ideas and feedback and so can be slotted into any timetable without too much inconvenience.

2. Team-building activities

The benefits of team-building exercises and cooperative learning activities in relation to developing peer relationships and classroom community are well known. They provide opportunities for individual students to develop communication skills, appreciate each other's strengths and capabilities and, most importantly in terms of community building, bond with each other.

Activities can be incorporated into lessons as aids to learning or can be scheduled as one-off lessons or starter activities. Time spent off curriculum on these activities is never wasted and will be paid back in terms of increased motivation, improved morale and better relationships.

To find suitable activities just Google the term **'team-building activities'**. Most activities of this nature have been designed for the corporate world but can be adapted to all areas of the curriculum with minimal modification. You should also endeavor to include cooperative learning activities in your lessons. Again, there are many websites providing free activities and these can be adapted to most curriculum topics.

Here's an example of a Team-Building Activity which can be adapted for almost any lesson topic. My students LOVED this activity.

Photo Scavenger Hunt

Time: Whole lesson - 60 minutes

Number of People: Any Size

Materials: Digital camera for each group or photos of scenes around the classroom/school depending on variation

Preparation:

Write up the Scavenger Hunt comprising of a series of staged photographs which teams must collect. Some examples might be: 'Form a letter of the alphabet with your bodies', 'show how particles are arranged in solids, liquids and gases', 'complete the practical experiment and take a photo of the equipment you use' etc.

Directions:

1. Divide group into teams of 4-6 people.

2. Hand out the Scavenger Hunt form.

3. Inform students of the expectations/restrictions. Some possibilities might be:

    a. Every group member must be in the picture except the photographer.

    b. The photographer must be different for every photo.

    c. Time limit=40 minutes.

    d. Stay as quiet as possible in the hallway.

    e. No entering any other classroom.

4. As the groups finish, download the pictures onto the computer.

5. View them as a group or set them up as a display in time for the next class period.

Variations:

1.Teams of students are provided with ONE photograph of a scene around the school/classroom – e.g. a specific notice board, fire extinguisher, stair case etc. The students identify the scene and find a topic-related question/task at the scene together with their next clue – another photo of a different scene.

Activities like this take time to set up but the rewards are huge. Getting your most challenging students interested in *any* activity in the classroom (even one not strictly related to the curriculum) is a tremendous first step in changing negative attitudes and once they see that the classroom can be interesting and enjoyable, you have a foundation for growth and further learning.

I've put together a few more activities in an info-sheet called '**Cooperative & Team-building Activities Samples**'. Just head on over to the resource page which accompanies this book.

http://needsfocusedteaching.com/kindle/transform/

Part 3

Satisfying the Need for Empowerment – Praise & Encouragement

We all know that young people given praise for positive behaviour are more likely to repeat that good behaviour and less inclined to seek attention in inappropriate ways. If there's one thing I'm sure of it's that there is not a child on the planet who, deep down, doesn't <u>want</u> to succeed; and if you're the one who consistently recognises their efforts and their successes they *will* respond to you.

Without doubt, one of the very best methods for getting *any* student on side is to show acknowledgement when they do something right, do something well, or manage to do something they have previously struggled with. But this is common sense, you already know this.

There have been countless studies on the effects of praise showing that levels of on-task behaviour increase as teachers' rates of praise increase and you'll have been told a million times that 'all you have to do to get kids to behave properly is simply to tell them how well they are doing when they do something right'.

So why doesn't it work?

Well, there is a lot more to effective praise than just saying 'well done' and in this section, I'm going to share with you some ideas for making this strategy *much* more effective and how you can *instantly* get students on your side. But first we need to first look at some of the reasons why praise *doesn't* always work as well as we intend:

Reason why praise doesn't always work # 1

Praise only really works if the person giving it is *respected* by the student they're praising.

If a member of staff has neither a high-perceived status in the school, nor the respect of the students, praise from them will have little positive effect. In fact, it can have the opposite effect and can even be seen as quite embarrassing. The obvious strategy in this case is to improve status and gain more respect by working on the key features in this report. Once a level of mutual respect has been reached, praise will more likely have the desired effect.

Reason why praise doesn't always work # 2

Some students just can't handle being praised in public.

On more than one occasion I've seen lovely pieces of work being torn up and ruined by the same student that created them simply because a staff member has congratulated them on their efforts. The way to avoid this is to offer praise privately, thereby avoiding peer pressure. Perhaps take the student to one side or catch them at the end of the lesson to have a quiet word. This has the added advantage of seeming to be more sincere because of the extra attention the child receives.

Excessive praise can have an *adverse* effect on students.

The 'anti-praise' lobby believe students can become *dependent* on the appreciation of adults and that praise therefore does little to develop confidence in their *own* abilities or their motivation to succeed. In this way, students who are lavishly over-praised for routine effort may opt for less challenging tasks - perhaps in fear of not succeeding, or perhaps in the knowledge that they will have praise heaped upon them anyway - even for minimum effort.

Equally, excessive praise can increase a student's apprehension in the face of new tasks and cause anxiety that they may not meet the teacher's expectations (*"Is my picture alright Miss Smith? Have I done this bit right Miss Smith?"*). Ultimately this will lead to tremendous disappointment if they fail and consequently receive less praise than they were hoping for.

To counteract these problems, teachers simply need to improve the QUALITY of the praise they use rather than the QUANTITY. Give sincere, genuine 1:1 praise when it is truly *justified* as opposed to the million-and-one throwaway "well done", "brilliant" and "very good" comments which are bandied around every classroom without a second thought.

Praise can actually encourage inappropriate behaviour.

This is interesting. Very often little concern is given to the driving factors which may lie beneath a students' behaviour and it is entirely possible to *reward* and *encourage* inappropriate behaviour which is prompted by ulterior motives.

Consider this example:

Let's say Jonny (known for his dramatic outbursts when provoked by classmates) is sitting quietly in class, and Big George is needling him with unsavoury comments about his mum.

On this occasion, Jonny displays remarkable self-control and manages to ignore Big George – partly because he is helped by Peter and Paul who both jump to his aid with positive comments: *"Just ignore him Jonny, he's just trying to wind you up"*.

Because mature behaviour like this needs to be acknowledged, the teacher praises both Peter and Paul for being so considerate and helping to avert what would normally have resulted in a messy scuffle between Jonny and George. But what if Peter was acting out of genuine concern for his friend Jonny's welfare and didn't want to see him get into trouble, whereas Paul was deliberately manipulating the teacher? What if Paul had been in trouble all week himself and had come to Jonny's aid purely to get in the teacher's good books.

In the above example both Paul and Peter received positive recognition. If the psychological belief that 'behaviour which is positively reinforced is more likely to be repeated' is true, then Peter will repeat caring, considerate behaviour and Paul will become increasingly manipulative.

That is quite an argument against praise but don't worry, it's not all bad news. I firmly believe 'praise and encouragement' is absolutely one of your most powerful preventive classroom management tools so let's look at some ideas to make it's done right...

Six Ways to Make Praise & Encouragement More Effective

Here are some ways of improving praise so that it creates the kind of positive changes you want to see in your challenging students...

Watery praise doesn't wash! If you want praise to work you've got to make it SPECIFIC.

Let's start by making a concerted effort to stop using wishy-washy praise comments like "well done", "excellent" and "very good". It's not that I've got anything against the words themselves, and I'm not saying they shouldn't be used but when they are handed out like candy in the classroom in a weak attempt to create a 'positive environment' I fully believe they are a complete waste of time.

The problem is that these comments are too <u>vague</u> and are often said without real <u>consideration</u>. *Real* praise – the kind that actually makes a difference - comes from genuinely noticing when a student puts effort into something or has managed to complete something they wouldn't normally manage to do. Giving thoughtful, specific recognition demonstrates that you are taking real notice in what they are doing – a throw away "well done" doesn't.

If you want to improve the behaviour of students using praise the comments you use must be in FULL recognition of what they've done right. By that I mean praise needs to be **SPECIFIC**.

You need to tell them exactly *what* they did and exactly *why* it was good. Like this...

"Jonny! Stand back and look at what you've done... this is a fantastic portrait! What really sets this apart is the way you've made that eye come to life by showing the light reflecting here. That really makes it look realistic. And the texture you've got on the hair is superb."

Here's another:

"Jonny, you've sat quietly for the last 10 minutes and got on with your work. That's great because I've been able to go and help other students and I haven't needed to speak at you or remind you to get on. Well done you've shown you can work independently!"

In summary, in both cases, by giving SPECIFIC praise, the teacher is telling the student <u>WHAT</u> they've done and <u>WHY</u> they should be pleased with themselves.

Effective Praise Enhancer # 2

Praise effort rather than achievement

By focusing on effort rather than achievement we can praise a student *even if they fail* - and that's very important. Waiting for a child to complete a task before praising them means missing out on untold opportunities to *encourage* them along the way.

If a friend was dieting you wouldn't wait until they had reached their target weight before making positive comments, would you? You'd help them along the way with encouragement, because acknowledging their effort helps them stick in and persevere and, importantly, can help them overcome or avoid frustration.

Here are a couple of ways you can praise EFFORT to encourage students in their efforts...

"Jonny, you are working really, really well on this. What you've done so far is spot on. Just keep going using the same technique and you'll have it done in no time."

"You've tried so hard on this Jonny; it's great to see you putting so much effort in - you've really showed tremendous determination and that's an important strength to develop."

Effective Praise Enhancer # 3

Avoid personal judgements

We've already discovered that praise can make some students dependent on the adult giving the praise and that they can modify their behaviour solely to please the teacher. This is particularly common when a statement of praise involving a personal judgement from the teacher is directed to a *power-oriented* student - when they see the person giving the praise as the person with all the power, there is a conflict.

Rather than judging students by telling them what *we* think of their efforts we should be encouraging them to reflect on their *own* efforts. The following statement illustrates what I mean:

`"I really like what you've done here"` ...is a personal judgment which encourages the student to be dependent on the view of the teacher whereas: `"You should be proud of what you've done here"` ...is more likely to encourage independence and self-motivation.

Effective Praise Enhancer # 4

If you want praise to change a child they've got to *feel* it - it has to be SINCERE.

Most students can recognise fake praise from a hundred yards away - and they *don't like it*. If you can't say it with honesty, it's best not to say anything at all. Remember: praise comes from the heart, flattery comes from the teeth.

Effective Praise Enhancer # 5

Be aware that praise is often more effective on a 1:1 basis

I know I've already mentioned this but it's worth repeating. Some students (a surprisingly large proportion) don't like receiving praise in front of other people. For whatever reason – some just can't accept compliments very well so you have more chance of your praise being well-received if you give it out of earshot of the rest of the students. Catch them on the way out of the door or call them over to a quiet corner of the room. Praise is much more sincere when it's a private affair.

Effective Praise Enhancer # 6

Make them reflect on their efforts

Some people lavish praise on students for literally anything and everything in the hope that a torrent of positive words will raise their self-esteem and motivate them.

But praise is more effective when we get students to stop and *reflect* on what they've done. By getting them to pause and think about their efforts we encourage them to recognise and evaluate the feelings associated with positive action. If they enjoy these feelings, there is more chance they will want to repeat the actions – *for themselves*, and not just to please someone else. One way we can do this is to simply ask a question about their efforts...

"Jonny stop and look at your work a minute. Tell me what you think of what you've done today."

"Hey Jonny, now that everything has settled down, how do you feel to have got over that difficult problem? What skills did you use to resolve it? How does it feel knowing that you can use those same skills next time you are confronted with a problem like this?"

Two Super-Powerful Praise Strategies

In addition to the usual method of praising a student – speaking to them directly - here are two more very powerful and effective praise strategies you might want to consider using in the classroom...

Super-Powerful Praise Strategy #1

Indirect praise

This is a great way to acknowledge a student's strengths, abilities and efforts without saying anything to them directly. Some students, as we know, find it difficult to accept praise directly – this gets around the problem. The idea is to make positive statements about a student *just* loud enough for them to hear but giving the impression that you are talking *about them* not *to them*.

The impression we want to convey in the examples below is that we hold Jonny in high esteem – so much so that we talk about him favourably to others.

"Go and ask Jonny about it – he's picked this up very quickly."

"Go and watch Jonny for a minute – he's brilliant at this and you can learn a lot from him."

"Mr Jones, have you noticed a change in Jonny lately? I've seen him make some really big changes in Maths – he's really trying."

Send letters home

This has such a positive impact on students - I only wish I'd started doing it earlier in my career.

Sending a short, positive letter home can transform a previously negative child - literally overnight - into one who is motivated and eager to please. This is also one method that works well even with older students, right up to age 16 and beyond. It is also very effective for students who don't accept public praise very well - a letter home means their friends will never find out!

Letters home can be 'quick-notes' or more formal, traditional letters on school headed paper. You can send out simple postcards for odd pieces of particularly good work or award 'extra special' letters in response to sustained effort.

Three Creative Positive Reinforcement (PR) Strategies You Might Not Have Thought Of

Positive reinforcement isn't just about praise and encouragement; it helps if there is some variety in the way you acknowledge appropriate student behaviours. With that in mind, here are a couple of 'creative' ideas for marking the moment...

Creative PR strategy #1

The victory dance.

Teach students to develop their own, personalised ten second 'Victory Dance'. Whenever you want to offer special praise to a student, clear a space at the front of the room (or install a podium if you have spare budget), pump up the bass and allow them their ten seconds of fame.

Creative PR strategy #2

Silent Cheers

Teach students to reward fellow class-members for good work and good behaviour with a silent cheer. Offer spot prizes for the most dramatic and convincing exhibition of silent applause.

This is particularly useful during exam periods or when the teacher in the neighbouring classroom has expressed concern about the amount of fun your classes seem to have.

The Staffroom Praise Board

This is a whole-school approach to building a positive working environment as well as helping develop positive relationships between all staff and students. It is based on the principal that individual students' efforts often get overlooked – particularly in a large setting. The strategy ensures that even the smallest improvements made by a particular student are noticed and acknowledged, potentially by EVERY member of staff.

Directions:

1. Assign an area of wall in the staffroom for the praise board. There should be room for five to ten A4 sheets and it should be an area which staff will see whenever they enter the staffroom.

2. Each week, students are nominated for a place on the praise board (they aren't told about this). Staff put forward a student and give reasons for their nomination. After a vote, a photo of each chosen student is put on the board together with a brief summary of why they have been chosen.

3. The idea is that every member of staff will see this board regularly throughout the course of the week. When they next see one of the students from the board – either in the classroom, in the dinner queue or out on the yard - they can mention how impressed they are with the student's achievement. Over the space of a week, a student will receive a huge amount of positive, and often much-needed, reinforcement with several members of staff acknowledging the same achievement.

"Hey Jonny, I hear you were very good in maths this week. Well done mate, keep it up!"

"Great work Jonny! A little bird told me you managed to get through a whole day without being sent out of a single lesson. Brilliant! Isn't it better when you're not getting detention every day?"

The Danger of Using Rewards

I just want to briefly mention the issue of rewards here because they are often considered, along with praise, to be an effective strategy for positively reinforcing good behaviour. The Needs Focused Approach™ doesn't advocate relying heavily on rewards to change inappropriate behaviour though for several reasons.

One of the main problems with reward programs is that they don't take into account students who lack the capacity or skills to complete a designated task or meet a required level of work – they just assume that the only reason they aren't working is because they don't *want* to do so.

Consider a boy who is offered rewards to bring in his homework. If he lives in an acutely chaotic home where school is viewed negatively by other family members and he has never been taught even the most basic of time management skills, the reward won't help him – it won't make his family members give him support, and it won't teach him the required organisational skills to find time to sit down to do his homework.

On the live version of our motivation course I use the promise of cash rewards for a series of impossible tasks to hammer this message home. Participants are offered increasingly valuable cash prizes if they manage to complete a series of puzzles. They can't do it. No matter how much they want to and no matter how much they would like to further deplete my bank account. It makes no difference how much I increase the potential prize money, they can't complete the task. If the skills are lacking, the reward won't help.

Another problem with rewards is that they provide, at best, only a *temporary* improvement. Once the treats (or the person giving the treats) have gone, the behaviour resumes. At worst, they help build and sustain a society of young people who will only do as they are asked as long as they are given something of value in return –

"Sure, I'll do as you ask but what are you going to give me in return?"

Our aim must be to TEACH appropriate behaviour and encourage students to behave appropriately for the right reasons and for the intrinsic rewards such behaviour brings - not just because they have been promised a treat or reward for doing so.

Now, I need to be clear, this doesn't mean we shouldn't give kids rewards now and again - we just have to get the *timing* right.

You see, when rewards are promised *in advance* ("Do this and I'll give you this") they are nothing more than bribes. But when they are *unexpected* and given *after* an increased effort or positive change in behaviour they can 'mark the moment' very well and reinforce the behaviour we want to see. Student effort *should* be recognised and celebrated – and rewards *can* be used to this end - but we can do better than to rely entirely on bribery where they are promised in advance of an achieved target, as is the case with most school reward systems.

The BEST Way to Use Rewards if You Want to See Positive Results... FAST

Here's a much better way to use rewards as true motivators: offer them *spontaneously* as...

...occasional surprises.

One of the most effective reward systems I ever saw in operation in a school worked entirely on this basis. Unlike most other centres and special schools I'd worked in for children with behaviour difficulties, there were no sticker charts and points totals on offer here. Instead, a youth worker was assigned to take students who had shown improved effort out on a trip. The 'trip' might be a run into town; a visit to a park or sports centre; an event or show; helping out with unpacking some deliveries; or even gardening. It all depended on the level of reward the teacher felt the students *deserved*.

The effectiveness of this lay in the method of delivery. The youth worker would walk into the classroom (this was pre-arranged with the teacher but unbeknown to the students) and say something along the lines of: *"Jonny, I hear you've been working very hard this week. I think you deserve to come out with me."*

The impact this had on the other students (and Jonny of course) was quite astounding. There was no build up nor expectation on the students" part, but good effort was still positively rewarded.

This approach was more about rejoicing in and celebrating achievement. The set up gave the opportunity for the teacher to say *"look what happens when you work hard"* and it was quite a profound moment for the other students to look up and see Jonny walk out of the room.

Individual spontaneous rewards are most effective when they mean something to the student. This is one reason why it is so important to get to know students and find out their hobbies and passions. It's obviously not as effective giving a sticker with a picture of an animal to a boy who is crazy about tractors, for example.

The following suggested spontaneous rewards can be adapted to fit any individual student's interests although some of them are applicable to younger students only.

Spontaneous Reward #1

Classroom privileges

These individual rewards may seem small and insignificant compared to the expensive tangible prizes – record vouchers, mobile phone vouchers etc. offered in some school reward systems but, if chosen wisely and delivered at the right time, in the right way, they can have a great effect.

"Jonny, you kept your temper today all the way through the lesson and completed the work I set you. You can have a cup of tea at break and first choice on activities."

☑ Sit at the teacher's desk

☑ Time on computer

☑ Be in line first for lunch (and/or can nominate a friend)

☑ Choose their seat for the day

☑ Help the secretary

☑ Help the librarian

☑ Classroom job - taking care of the class animal/s, being in charge of materials/supplies, watering plants, taking the register, operating the projector, maintaining the calendar, cleaning the board etc.

☑ Take a class game home for the night

☑ Keep a favourite soft toy/class mascot on your desk

☑ Use the couch or beanbag chair

☑ Set up a classroom display

☑ Get a fun worksheet from the 'fun pile'

Spontaneous Reward #2

Special awards and trophies

Awards are almost always used in classrooms in the form of certificates, but why stop there? A trophy is far more appealing – even if it is just a flimsy, plastic joke 'Oscar' – and it doesn't have to be something they take home; it's the recognition and the ceremony that counts. A very brief, simple, humorous, surprise award ceremony can take place at the end of the week or once a month/term to highlight students' progress in any given area:

☑ This week's 'Independent Worker' award goes to... (suggested joke trophy: Toy plastic workman figure)

☑ This week's 'Early Finisher' award goes to... (suggested joke trophy: Toy plastic watch)

☑ This week's 'Most Improved Student' is... (suggested joke trophy: Rosette, 'thumbs-up' certificate or model)

Whole-class rewards

Individual spontaneous rewards are very powerful but this same approach can also be adapted for a whole group – with tremendous benefits in terms of improved social interaction between students and an enhanced community feeling.

Occasional, unannounced *"just because you've all been working so hard"* whole class treats such as videos (with popcorn) or cakes and soft drinks go a long way to motivating a previously disengaged group and can help students see that we recognise their efforts.

And while we're on the subject of spontaneous treats I want to tell you about a little gift we've included with this mini-course – a very quirky reward you can give your students when they do something extra special...

The £Million Behaviour Note (also available in Dollars) is a cool reward you might want to give out now and again when your students surprise you for the right reasons. Like any reward the novelty value will wear out over time but you might just find, for a while at least, that these little slips of paper will make you very popular and give you a new lease of power in the classroom! :-)

BONUS TOOL: Fun Reward – Millionaire Bank Notes

You can download a free set of Million Pound/ Dollar/Euro notes for photocopying here:

http://needsfocusedteaching.com/kindle/transform/

Part 4

Satisfying the Need for Empowerment - Routines

Continuing with the topic of empowering our students, here's another way to meet this need by making it easy for them to do the right thing, so that there's more likelihood of them succeeding in your lessons.

I should also point out that this method can *dramatically* reduce your workload and stress. It will also reduce the constant need to repeat instructions and will practically *automate* your classroom.

How is all this possible? Simply by establishing and using simple *classroom routines* on a daily basis. Routines really are among the most powerful preventive techniques in your toolbox.

One of the reasons why routines are so effective is because they let students know *exactly* what they have to do in any given situation by giving them a clear, step-by-step method to follow. And because this method doesn't change, the routine creates total *consistency*.

Let me show you what I mean with this simple example. Let's assume the end of a lesson is approaching. The teacher knows exactly what she wants the students to do – get cleared away as quickly as possible - and she issues the instruction to do so.

Question: Which of these instructions will give her the greatest chance of success?

a) "The bell is about to ring, everyone. Put everything away and get ready to be dismissed please... Come on everyone... Quickly now... Let's get packed away... HURRY UP!"

b) "Okay, the bell will ring in 5 minutes, it's time to clear away. You know what to do." (The teacher points to a clearly displayed, and well-practised, routine posted at the front of the classroom – see below).

End of Lesson Routine

- Put textbooks on the shelf and exercise books on my desk

- Put all equipment back where you got it from

- Put all rubbish in the bin

- Clear your desk

- Sit in silence facing the front

- If it is the last period of the day, stack the chairs by the back wall.

If the correct answer isn't obvious, go and sit at the back of the class.

OK, the first set of instructions *could* have the desired effect with a well behaved, well trained, considerate class – but if we always had that type of class you wouldn't be reading this. With most groups it will probably result in a somewhat chaotic scene with some students continuing to sit and chat, and some taking it as a cue for mass hysteria, with perhaps a few actually tidying the room.

Vague instructions, more often than not, give rise to vague *results* because they don't give the students clear enough direction. But it's not just about making the classroom run more efficiently – routines also help with behaviour. Vague directions give lively students an excuse to misbehave as there are too many variables when they aren't told *exactly* what to do. They will wander, play dumb, claim they 'didn't know what they were supposed to do' and find something else to occupy them.

As a result, what should be a simple job degenerates into the time-consuming and stressful task of dealing with multiple behaviour issues, with you the teacher becoming increasingly frustrated as time ticks by without students doing what you wanted them to. You will find yourself repeating instructions, shouting, yelling and having to deal with progressively more problems from students who choose not to follow instructions.

Option 'b)' works because the teacher has already spent time teaching her students the *routine* for 'the end of the lesson'. There is no need for confusion or wasted time. No need to repeat instructions, no need to check that everyone has understood and give extra prompts to those who haven't – everyone knows *exactly* what to do, and the teacher gets to watch contentedly as they do it.

In the same way that the 'end of lesson' routine reduces problems at the end of the lesson, routines can be used for almost every transition or behaviour 'hot spot' throughout the school day. Indeed, routines can be set up for virtually any and every troublesome time or activity in the classroom such as these:

- Entering classroom

- Start of the lesson

- Distributing materials

- Clearing away materials

- Asking for help

- Transition between activities or tasks

- What to do when you've finished your task

- What to do when you're late

- Using certain equipment

- Group work

- Going to the library

- Watching a video

- Listening to an outside speaker/visitor

- Answering questions

- Handing in work

- Handing in homework

- Leaving classroom

- Etc.

How much easier would your teaching day be if you had routines in place for all

those tricky times and lesson 'hot spots' listed above? How much smoother would the lesson be if your students knew *exactly* what to do in each of those circumstances?

The key is to make lots of routines – as you need. Teach them, practice them, sing them if you want, but make them *habitual* and put them up on walls as reminders - so that all you have to do with slowcoaches and avoiders is simply lift a finger and point at the sign on the wall... "*What should you be doing?*"

There are a couple of important points to remember with regard to routines before we move on from this section. Firstly, be sure to only introduce one routine at a time. You will overwhelm and confuse your students if you try to force too many rules on them at once.

And secondly, there will always be students who won't buy in and won't follow the routine when you ask them to. What do we do in response to this? Well, first of remember that asking students to do what you want them to can be difficult if you don't first put in place the *'preventive strategies'* that we cover in the rest of this mini-guide. Positive relationships, praise, satisfying needs etc. all play a crucial role in getting respect and compliance from your toughest groups.

But for those who *still* refuse to follow routines we use consequences. These, like everything else I'm introducing here, are dealt with in detail in my main book **Take Control of the Noisy Class** but as a treat, I'd like to give you a sample of one of my videos which explains the process of using stepped consequences in response to students who won't follow instructions. To get this video, head over to the free resources page; I hope you find it useful!

http://needsfocusedteaching.com/kindle/transform/

Note:

I must stress this point - reaching for a consequence in immediate response to inappropriate behaviour is not nearly as effective as spending time teaching routines in the first place.

Part 5

Satisfying the Need for Empowerment – Clear Instructions

In this section, we're going to look at how we can communicate with students so that they actually listen to, and follow, our instructions.

We are going to look at two key methods:

1. Being Congruent

2. Making sure instructions are clear & unambiguous

1. Being congruent

The first aspect of cutting out arguments associated with the instructions we give our students concerns the *way* in which we actually communicate them. In terms of communication, *congruence* is about making sure the messages we give through our facial expressions, body language and voice tone/pitch/volume clearly match the words we use and help convey our message without being misinterpreted.

It is difficult to be aware and maintain control of body language, facial expressions etc. when dealing with confrontation but the *way* we speak to an angry or frustrated student is *at least* as important as the actual words we use and has a tremendous impact on the outcome.

A student will read everything about our approach, our stance and the way we look at them before we actually start to speak and if we get any of these crucial aspects wrong they will have decided to either listen, switch off or retaliate before we even open our mouths. It is the silent messages we unconsciously give that are often at the root of students either ignoring or arguing with us.

Does our weary expression, slouched posture and exasperated tone give them the message that we're *tired* and *worn out*? If we do there's a good chance they'll either ignore us or push a little harder to tip us over the edge when we ask them to do something they'd rather not.

Do our folded arms, accusational tone of voice and frown give them the message that we don't like them? If we do they might well turn against us completely. Tough students might retaliate there and then while quieter members might hold a grudge and seek retribution at a later date. In either case, they are unlikely to behave as we would like.

The _way_ we give instructions has a massive impact on _how_ students respond to them. We can give the impression that we are a pushover, a threat or a leader depending on the silent messages we give out so if you find your students aren't responding to your instructions in the way you'd like this might be a good area to reflect on.

If you are interested in using your body language as well as other 'silent' communication tools such as NLP anchors to manage your classroom I've got another great bonus for you.

A few years ago, I spent many months interviewing over 30 expert teachers and education authors on various aspects of pedagogy, lesson delivery and classroom management and I'd like to give you one of the recordings free because it relates specifically to what we're talking about here.

Pearl Nitsche is an expert in using NLP in the classroom and she delivered a wonderful presentation on non-verbal classroom management. It's a real eye opener and contains some very powerful  strategies for running your classroom almost on auto-pilot. I used to sell this recording at £25 but you can have it as a gift when you visit the resources page:

http://needsfocusedteaching.com/kindle/transform/

2. Making instructions <u>clear</u> and <u>unambiguous</u>

The clearer the directions, the more chance there is that they will do what we want and the less chance there is for arguments due to misinterpretation.

"Jonny, you need to stop tapping your pen, sit properly on your chair and look this way."

...will have more chance of getting the desired outcome than...

"Jonny, stop it!"

A request like this immediately leaves us open to questions...

"Stop what?"

...and then before we know it, an argument has developed...

"I wasn't doing anything! You're always picking on me!"

Etc.

Once they've drawn you into a 'battle-of-wills' your lesson is lost.

Here's another simple example...

"Get on with your work quietly"

The word *'quietly'* means different things to different people so straight away we have

opened the door to confrontation. For one student, it means *'whispering'* while for another it means *'talking in their normal speaking voice'*. Another student might take this as meaning there is no real rule on noise levels at all. In each case, the students who is challenged for making too much noise will almost certainly protest that they are "working quietly". It's not surprising that vague instructions like this don't always result in the behaviour we want to see and are often a source of arguments.

To make sure the students keep within the noise levels we want all we need to do is clarify exactly what we mean by 'quietly'.

Younger children might need a <u>tangible representation</u> of the word – they could be shown a ruler and told to use their **'30cm voices'** or their **'partner voices'** instead of their **'yard voices'**.

For older students, we might simply clarify our instruction by demonstrating the volume we are referring to. Of course, there is more to giving instructions than this and in my book, Take Control of the Noisy Class I go into the subject in much more detail. Hopefully!

Part 6

Satisfying the Need for FUN –
Making Lessons More
Engaging

For some teachers, the idea of having to make lessons fun just so that disengaged students might take a bit more interest doesn't sit too well. Their opinion is that one of the most important things young people should learn is this:

'Life isn't always fun and there are times you just have to get on with it. You are in school to learn, not waste your time having fun.'

It's true of course - children go to school to *learn*. Most people, therefore, would agree with the above statement... and so do I. But only to a certain extent; let me explain...

Many years ago, at the start of my teaching career, I attended an interview for a post working with a group of children with Special Educational Needs at a prestigious high school in Cumbria. The formal interview was held in the afternoon but before that I had to teach a demonstration lesson – I was nervous under scrutiny, naturally, but by the end I was reasonably happy with my performance.

After lunch, I was grilled by the panel that consisted of the Head Teacher, four senior teachers, and two governors. The Head was a particularly charismatic man with a cheerful, welcoming manner which helped soothe my interview nerves, but when it was his turn to question me he held his chin thoughtfully, paused and peered down his nose at me, just long enough to leave me feeling like a specimen under a microscope. Unease stirred within me.

"I've got some *excellent* teachers at this school, Mr Plevin," he said. In my mind, I was already thanking them for their time as my optimism began to drain away, and I was convincing myself that my teaching style hadn't impressed him. "Yes, *excellent* teachers. But do you know what? *Not one of them* could do what you just did in that classroom with those students. The way you held the attention of that group was exceptional."

I'd have been less surprised if he'd hit me with a sock full of custard. Actually, I was embarrassed if truth be known and I looked in astonishment at their smiling faces. But he hadn't finished.

"However..." His tone changed as he put his hands on his knees and fixed me with a

searching stare. "What I want to know is... just what did those children actually *learn*? There's no doubt you can *entertain* my students, but what did you actually *teach* them?" I realised his opening praise had been directed at my ability as an entertainer, not a teacher.

He was dead right of course, and his question had knocked me sideways. My philosophy up to that point had been based on *entertaining* the students in my classroom – after all, if they are engaged and not even the difficult kids are giving me behaviour headaches, then the lesson *must* be a success... right? And suddenly, in the middle of that interview, I found my skills and values under close scrutiny. To cut a long story short I *was* offered a job at that school – but not the one I had applied for! I was offered an entirely different role leading a newly created department and... *I turned it down.*

I remember clearly the look on the face of that noble and passionate Head Teacher as he said to me "When would you be able to start?" and I replied "I'm sorry, I'm afraid I will have to decline your kind offer. As a result of this interview I'm going to go and reassess my career." Without intending to he had, in a few minutes, changed my entire self-image! We chatted for some time and parted on good terms. I often think back to that day because it marked a turning point for me. It taught me a lesson that led to me changing the way I teach, and has undoubtedly been a contributory factor in the development of my business.

Making lessons fun *isn't* enough to stop behaviour problems, and it isn't going to miraculously transform your challenging students into hard-working, diligent stars. Without knowledge, understanding and application of other key teaching and classroom management skills a *fun* lesson with challenging students may well turn into a free-for-all and only serve to build you a reputation as a walk-over. Instead, the aim should be to improve *all* aspects of your lesson delivery and content. Yes, there will be *fun*. Kids like to have fun and when learning is fun studies have found it to be more successful. But in addition to fun we'll be making lessons *relevant*, making them *interactive*, making them *memorable*, making them more *engaging*. We will take steps to ensure that *all* your learners are adequately catered for and fully involved in the learning process.

I like to use the simple analogy of your students each carrying an 'emotion rucksack' on their backs as they enter your lessons. If they arrive with the feeling that the lesson, based on their previous experience, is something they will have to *endure* for the next hour – something boring, irrelevant to them, perhaps embarrassing or difficult – their rucksack will be filled with *negative* emotions before they even set foot in the room.

Teaching students who have preconceived negativity towards your lessons is the hard way to teach. It's very difficult getting them to engage when they have already made up their minds that the lesson isn't something they're going to enjoy or get any benefit from. The *easy* way is to have them actually looking forward to the lesson and carrying a rucksack with a little bit of *intrigue*, perhaps recollections of a few *laughs* they had last lesson, or a feeling of *success* and *achievement* at having understood a difficult concept for the first time.

To help you on your quest to provide stimulating lessons and satisfy your students' need for fun I've provided you with a free report today packed with activities that will help you make your lessons more engaging and appealing. Remember, when your students find your lessons engaging, interesting and fun, there is far less chance that they will need to find their *own* fun by misbehaving!

BONUS TOOL: Engaging Lesson Activities (PDF Report)

An exciting collection of our most novel, quirky, attention-grabbing starters, plenaries, fill-ins and classroom activities to make your lessons active and FUN. Your students will LOVE these!

Signup for your FREE downloadable resources to get this bonus tool:

http://needsfocusedteaching.com/kindle/transform/

Sadly, this is the end of our time here. Sniff. But don't worry! If you've enjoyed what you've read here (and 'watched' – assuming you've had a look at the bonus video), you will find my main book Take Control of the Noisy Class very useful (See next section).

Each of the strategies mentioned here is explained in much more detail and there are masses of additional tips and techniques for getting the most from your most challenging students.

Closing

Take Control of The Noisy Class

To get your copy, go here:

https://www.amazon.co.uk/Take-Control-Noisy-Class-Super-effective/dp/1785830082/

Also, if you'd like to receive my FREE **Behaviour Tips** on an inconsistent and irregular basis via my email service, just sign up for your free book resources and you'll start receiving my Behaviour Tips.

http://needsfocusedteaching.com/kindle/transform/

These tips serve as the perfect accompaniment to the mini-course because they contain short, practical ideas and strategies for responding to all kinds of inappropriate classroom behaviour, as well as some handy teaching tips and ideas for improving student engagement. You'll get a repeat of the main ideas included in this book followed by short tutorials as text emails - as well as links to videos and further resources. All this will be sent direct to your email inbox once or twice a week, along with occasional notifications about some of our other products, special offers etc.

Obviously, you can opt out of this service any time you wish but in our experience, most people pick up a lot of *wonderful* ideas from these emails. And feel free to forward the messages and resources on to other teachers (staff meetings, staff room, pop them into your Christmas cards etc.).

Just remember to look out for emails from '***Needs Focused Teaching***' so that you don't miss all the goodies.

"Thanks a million. As a fresh teacher, I find this invaluable."

"Finally something concrete and applicable in real life – I've had enough of the people who have never set their foot in a real classroom but know how everything should be done in theory. Thanks a million. As a fresh teacher, I find this invaluable."

Jasna (Take Control of the Noisy Class customer)

Final Reminder!

 If you haven't already done so, head on over to the FREE resources page:

http://needsfocusedteaching.com/kindle/transform/

Where you'll find, amongst other things:

- Engaging Lesson Activities (PDF Report)

- '5 Ways to Show Students You Care'

- 'Cooperative & Team-building Activities Samples'.

- Record card questionnaire

- Fun Reward – Millionaire Bank Notes

- Bonus video (How to use consequences)

- Pearl Nitsche , webinar presentation

And that link again:

http://needsfocusedteaching.com/kindle/transform/

One more thing... Please help me get this book to as many teachers as possible, by leaving an honest review...

"I have seen nothing short of miracles occur."

"I have seen nothing short of miracles occur. My students' attitudes and behaviours have improved; they are excited and personally involved in their educational experience! What more could I ask? My E books have become my bible!!! I truly am a disciple!!!!! Love you guys."

Dawn (NeedsFocusedTeaching customer)

Review Request

If you enjoyed this book and can see the benefits to be had from using the Needs Focused Approach™ to prevent and reduce behaviour problems in your classroom, please leave me an honest review! Your support really does matter and it really does make a difference. I do read all the reviews so I can get your feedback and I do make changes as a result of that feedback.

If you'd like to leave a review, then all you need to do is go to the review section on the book's Amazon page. You'll see a big button that states "Write a customer review". Click on that and you're good to go!

You can also use the following links to locate the book on Amazon:

https://www.amazon.co.uk/dp/B072MJR85T

https://www.amazon.com/dp/B072MJR85T

For all other countries, please head over to the relevant Amazon site and either search for the book title or simply copy and paste the following code in the Amazon search bar to be taken directly to the book:

B072MJR85T

Have fun and thanks for your support...

Rob

"...your strategies work wonders!"

"Thank you so much Rob for what you are doing for the profession, your strategies work wonders! I have never tried the 'pen' but will do next time! Seriously speaking, I give the link to your productions to many young teachers I know because they are so unhappy sometimes and they need help which they find with what you do! So, thanks again and carry on with your good job!"

Marie (Take Control of the Noisy Class customer)

Suggested resource providers

Name: HowtoLearn.com and HowtoLearn.teachable.com

Specialty: Personalized Learning Assessments, Learning Solutions, Courses for Teachers, Parents and Students.

Website: www.HowtoLearn.com

Details: Online since 1996, the brainchild of best-selling author and college professor, Pat Wyman, known as America's Most Trusted Learning Expert. We invite you to become part of our global community and closed Facebook group. Your Learning Questions Answered at http://www.HowtoLearn.com/your-learning-questions-answered.

Resources: Take our Free Learning Styles Quiz at HowtoLearn.com and check out parent/teacher tested and approved courses at HowtoLearn.teachable.com.

* * *

Name: Time Savers for Teachers (Stevan Krajnjan)

Speciality: Resources guaranteed to save you time.

Website: http://www.timesaversforteachers.com/ashop/affiliate.php?id=7

Details: Popular forms, printable and interactive teacher resources that save time. Stevan Krajnjan was presented with an Exceptional Teacher Award by The Learning Disabilities Association of Mississauga and North Peel in recognition for outstanding work with children who have learning disabilities.

Resources: www.timesaversforteachers.com

* * *

Name: Nicola Morgan (NSM Training & Consultancy).

Speciality: Innovative resources to motivate staff and empower schools.

Website: www.nsmtc.co.uk

Details: NSM Training & Consultancy provides high quality training for teaching/non teaching staff in the UK and internationally. We provide a large range of courses, expert consultancy and guidance, publications, conferences as well as innovative resources to motivate staff and empower schools.

Resources: http://www.nsmtc.co.uk/resources/

* * *

Name: Susan Fitzell

Speciality: Special Education Needs

Website: www.SusanFitzell.com

Details: Seminar Handouts and supplemental resources for Differentiated Instruction, Motivation, Special Education Needs, Co-teaching, and more.

Resources: http://downloads.susanfitzell.com/

* * *

Name: Patricia Hensley

Speciality: Special Education

Website: http://successfulteaching.net

Details: Strategies and ideas for all grade levels. Great resource for new and struggling teachers.

Resources: Free Student Job Description. https://successfulteaching.blogspot.com/2007/10/student-job-description.html

*   *   *

Name: Julia G. Thompson

Speciality: Educational consultant, writer, and presenter.

Website: www.juliagthompson.com.

Details: Author of The First-Year Teacher's Survival Guide, Julia G Thompson specializes in assisting new teachers learn to thrive in their new profession.

Resources: For 57 free forms and templates to make your school year easier, just click go to her website and click on the Professional Binder page

*   *   *

Name: Steve Reifman

Speciality: Teaching the Whole Child (Empowering Classroom Management & Improving Student Learning)

Website: www.stevereifman.com

Details: National Board Certified Elementary Teacher & Amazon Best-Selling Author.

Author of '10 Steps to Empowering Classroom Management: Build a Productive, Cooperative Culture Without Using Rewards'

Resources: https://www.youtube.com/user/sreifman (FREE, 1-2 minute videos with tips for teachers & parents)

* * *

Name: Dave Vizard

Speciality: Behaviour Management

Website: www.behavioursolutions.com

Details: Creator of Brain Break materials and Ways to Manage Challenging Behaviour ebook.

Resources: www.behavioursolutions.myshopify.com/pages/brain-breaks

* * *

Name: Marjan Glavac

Specialty: Tips on getting a teaching job (resume, cover letter, interviews); classroom management strategies.

Website: www.thebusyeducator.com

Details: Marjan Glavac is a best selling motivational author, engaging speaker and elementary classroom teacher with over 29 years of teaching experience.

Resources: Free weekly newsletter, 4 free eBooks (http://thebusyeducator.com/homepage.htm)

* * *

Name: Dr. Rich Allen

Specialty: Workshops and keynotes on engagement strategies for students of all ages

Website: greenlighteducation.net

Details: Author of 'Green Light Teaching' and 'The Rock 'n Roll Classroom'

Resources: Please join our Teaching tips community and access lots of free resources and ideas for your classroom by clicking HERE.

* * *

Name: Ross Morrison McGill

Speciality: Managing director at TeacherToolkit Ltd.

Website: https://www.teachertoolkit.co.uk/

Details: Ross Morrison McGill is a deputy headteacher working in an inner-city school in North London. He is the Most Followed Teacher on Twitter in the UK and writes the Most Influential Blog on Education in the UK.

Resources: https://www.amazon.co.uk/Ross-Morrison-McGill/e/B00G33GTEO/ref=dp_byline_cont_book_1

What people say about us

"Even if you have never had "the class from hell", there is something here for you"

"As a PGCE student it is great to have the opportunity to pick up user-friendly and easily accessible information. The 'Behaviour Needs' course provides exactly that. In a series of amusing, creative, fast-paced sections, Rob Plevin builds up a staggering amount of practical and thought provoking material on classroom behaviour management. All of which are easily translated back in the classroom. Even if you have never had "the class from hell", there is something here for you and the follow up information from the website is laden with golden nuggets which will give you loads more ideas and interventions."

Steve Edwards (Workshop Attendee and Take Control of the Noisy Class customer)

* * *

"I want you to know that you have changed the lives of 40 of my students."

"What an informative day. The sessions on positive reinforcement and the importance of relationships were particularly memorable. I want you to know that you have changed the lives of 40 of my students. Thank you!"

Joanne W. (Singapore Workshop Attendee)

* * *

"...We will be inviting Rob back on every possible occasion to work with all of our participants and trainees."

"We were delighted to be able to get Rob Plevin in to work with our Teach First participants. From the start his dynamic approach captivated the group and they were enthralled throughout. Rob covered crucial issues relating to behaviour management thoroughly and worked wonders in addressing the participants' concerns about teaching in some of the most challenging schools in the country. We will be inviting Rob back on every possible occasion to work with all of our participants and trainees."

Terry Hudson, (Regional Director 'Teach First', Sheffield Hallam University)

* * *

"Thank you for helping me to be in more control."

"Rob, thank you very much for sharing your experience and reminding of these simple but effective things to do. Students' behaviour (or actually my inability to control it) is so frustrating that at times it feels that nothing can help. Thank you for helping me to be in more control."

Natasha Grydasova (*Take Control of the Noisy Class* customer)

* * *

"I am HAPPILY spending my Sat afternoon listening, watching and reading all your extremely helpful information!"

"Thank You Rob! What a wealth of excellent ideas! This is my 30th year teaching! You would think after 30 years teaching that I wouldn't need to be viewing your awesome videos and reading your helpful blog and website. However, I am HAPPILY spending my Sat afternoon listening, watching and reading all your extremely helpful information! Thank You So Much! I will be one of your biggest fans from now on!"

Kelly Turk (Needs Focused Video Pack customer)

* * *

"...terrific for those teachers who are frustrated."

"Great easy-to-listen-to video tips that will be terrific for those teachers who are frustrated. I'm forwarding this email on to the principals in my district right away!"

Sumner price (Take Control of the Noisy Class customer)

* * *

"Many thanks for all these really helpful life-savers!"

"Very many thanks. I have given myself trouble by letting kids into the room in a restless state with inevitable waste of teaching time. Your advice on calming them down in a positive, non-confrontational way and building rapport is very timely. Many thanks for all these really helpful life-savers!"

Philip Rozario (Take Control of the Noisy Class customer)

* * *

"Fantastic way to create a calm and secure learning environment for all the students."

"Thanks so much Rob. Fantastic way to create a calm and secure learning environment for all the students. It's great how you model the way we should interact with the students – firmly but always with respect."

Marion (Take Control of the Noisy Class customer)

* * *

"I will be recommending that the teachers in training that I deal with should have a look at these videos."

These tips and hints are put in a really clear, accessible fashion. As coordinator of student teachers in my school, I will be recommending that the teachers in training that I deal with should have a look at these videos.

Deb (Take Control of the Noisy Class customer)

* * *

"I found Rob Plevin's workshop just in time to save me from giving up."

"I found Rob Plevin's workshop just in time to save me from giving up. It should be compulsory – everybody in teaching should attend a Needs-Focused workshop and meet the man with such a big heart who will make you see the important part you can play in the lives of your most difficult students."

Heather Beames (Workshop Attendee)

* * *

"...the ideas, strategies and routines shared with our teachers have led to improved classroom practice."

"The Needs Focused Behaviour Management workshops in support of teacher training in Northern Ireland have been very well received and the ideas, strategies and routines shared with our teachers have led to improved classroom practice. This has been validated by both inspections at the University and observations of teachers."

Celia O'Hagan, (PGCE Course Leader, School of Education, University of Ulster)

* * *

"I have never enjoyed a course, nor learnt as much as I did with Rob."

"What a wonderfully insightful, non-patronising, entertainingly informative day. I have never enjoyed a course, nor learnt as much as I did with Rob. I was so impressed that I am recommending our school invite Rob along to present to all the staff so that we can all benefit from his knowledge, experience and humour."

Richard Lawson-Ellis (Workshop Attendee)

* * *

"...since I started following the principles in your materials, I have seen a vast improvement."

"Hi Rob, I would just like to say that since I started following the principles in your materials, I have seen a vast improvement. I had to teach a one hour interview lesson yesterday and was told that they thought the lesson was super and they loved my enthusiasm! I got the job!

Diane Greene (_Take Control of the Noisy Class customer_)

* * *

"Thanks to you, students from 30 some schools are truly engaged and not throwing pencils at the sub!"

Rob, Your student engagement series has been out of this world. I've already used various techniques as a substitute and students said I was **the best sub ever.** Thanks to you, students from 30 some schools are truly engaged and not throwing pencils at the sub!"

Leslie Mueller (Student Engagement Formula customer)

*   *   *

"So often professional development training is a waste of time; you may get one little gem from a whole day of training. You've given numerous strategies in 5 minutes."

Wow! So many people have gained so much from your videos! Teachers are time poor. A quick grab of effective ideas is what we all need. So often professional development training is a waste of time; you may get one little gem from a whole day of training. You've given numerous strategies in 5 minutes. Thanks for your generosity.

Mary – Ann (Take Control of the Noisy Class customer)

Made in the USA
San Bernardino, CA
01 April 2018